MASTERING THE ART OF SALES
STRATEGIES FOR BUILDING LASTING CUSTOMER RELATIONSHIPS

MASTERING THE ART OF SALES
STRATEGIES FOR BUILDING LASTING CUSTOMER RELATIONSHIPS

CARL BOTT

Amazon Publishing

Published in the United States by Amazon Publishing

ISBN 9798385977697

First Edition

CONTENTS

Chapter 1: Introduction to Sales
Sales is the lifeblood of any business, and it's one of the most critical skills you can possess. In this chapter, we'll dive into the basics of sales, including what it is, why it's important, and how you can master it.

Chapter 2: Setting Goals in Sales
One of the essential steps in mastering sales is setting goals. In this chapter, we'll discuss how to set clear and achievable goals that will motivate you and keep you focused on your objectives.

Chapter 3: Prospecting for Sales
Prospecting is the process of finding potential customers for your product or service. In this chapter, we'll explore different ways to find and connect with your target audience, including social media, email, and cold calling.

Chapter 4: Qualifying Prospects
Qualifying prospects is the process of determining if a potential customer is a good fit for your product or service. In this chapter, we'll discuss the critical questions to ask to qualify prospects, and how to identify their pain points and needs.

Chapter 5: Building Rapport

Building rapport is the foundation of any successful sales relationship. In this chapter, we'll dive into the art of building trust and rapport with your prospects, including how to communicate effectively and build a connection that will set you apart from the competition.

Chapter 6: Presenting Your Offer

Once you've built a rapport with your prospect, it's time to present your offer. In this chapter, we'll discuss the most effective ways to present your product or service, including how to handle objections and close the deal.

Chapter 7: Following Up

Following up is critical to closing the deal and building long-term relationships with your customers. In this chapter, we'll discuss the importance of following up, different ways to follow up, and how to keep the conversation going.

Chapter 8: Upselling and Cross-selling

Upselling and cross-selling are powerful techniques that can increase your sales revenue and improve customer satisfaction. In this chapter, we'll explore how to identify upselling and cross-selling opportunities and how to execute them effectively.

Chapter 9: Negotiation Strategies

Negotiation is an essential skill for sales professionals, and it can make or break a deal. In this chapter, we'll discuss negotiation strategies, including how to prepare for negotiations, how to handle objections, and how to close the deal.

Chapter 10: Developing a Sales Mindset

Finally, in this chapter, we'll explore the importance of developing a sales mindset. We'll discuss how to cultivate a positive attitude, how to stay motivated, and how to overcome obstacles and achieve success in sales.

CHAPTER 1
Introduction to Sales

Sales is the foundation of any successful business. It's the process of persuading and convincing potential customers to buy a product or service. Without sales, a business cannot survive, and this is why mastering sales is one of the most important skills you can possess.

Many people have a negative perception of sales, believing it to be pushy, manipulative, and dishonest. However, this couldn't be further from the truth. Successful sales professionals are skilled communicators, problem solvers, and relationship builders. They understand the needs and pain points of their customers and offer solutions that add value to their lives.

In today's fast-paced, competitive world, the ability to sell is more critical than ever. Whether you're a business owner, entrepreneur, or sales professional, you need to have a solid understanding of sales principles and techniques to succeed. Sales is not just about closing deals; it's about building relationships, solving problems, and adding value. It's about understanding your customer's needs and delivering solutions that exceed their expectations.

In the following chapters, we'll dive deeper into the world of sales, discussing everything from setting goals to developing a sales mindset. Whether you're just starting in sales or looking to improve your skills, this ebook will provide you with valuable insights and strategies to help you achieve success in your sales career.

CHAPTER 2
Setting Goals in Sales

To be successful in sales, you need to have clear and achievable goals. Goals provide you with a direction, a sense of purpose, and a roadmap to success. Without goals, you're like a ship without a rudder, drifting aimlessly with no destination in sight.

So, how do you set effective goals in sales? Here are some tips:

1. Be specific: Your goals should be specific and measurable. Instead of setting a vague goal like "increase sales," set a specific goal like "increase sales by 20% in the next quarter."

2. Set large goals: Strive for failure, as this is how you will learn and grow. If your goals are too easy, you won't be motivated to achieve them. Put the pieces in place to achieve a much larger goal making your smaller goals inevitable.

3. Write them down: Write down your goals and review them regularly. This will help you stay focused and motivated, and remind you of what you're working towards. Once a year in January is not enough! Be sure to check your goals daily if you want to succeed.

4. Break them down: Break your goals down into smaller, more manageable steps. This will make them less overwhelming and easier to achieve. Reverse engineer by taking your total goal and figuring what your hourly rate needs to become.

5. Be flexible: Be open to adjusting your goals as you go along. If you find that a goal is no longer relevant or achievable, don't be afraid to revise it.

Setting goals is not just about achieving sales targets; it's about personal growth and development. When you set and achieve goals, you gain confidence, learn new skills, and become more resilient. This is why it's important to set both short-term and long-term goals that challenge you and push you out of your comfort zone.

In conclusion, setting goals is a critical step in mastering sales. It provides you with a roadmap to success and helps you stay motivated and focused on your objectives. By following these tips, you can set effective goals that will help you achieve success in your sales career.

CHAPTER 3

Prospecting for Sales

Prospecting is the process of identifying and qualifying potential customers who may be interested in your product or service. It's a crucial step in the sales process because without qualified leads, you won't have anyone to sell to.

Here are some effective strategies for prospecting:

1. Define your target audience: Before you start prospecting, you need to define your ideal customer. This includes demographics, interests, pain points, and buying habits. The more specific you can be, the easier it will be to identify potential leads.

2. Use social media: Social media platforms like LinkedIn, Facebook, and Instagram are great tools for prospecting. You can search for potential customers based on keywords, job titles, and industry. You can also engage with prospects by commenting on their posts or sending them direct messages.

3. Attend events: Attend industry events, conferences, and trade shows to meet potential customers in person. This is an excellent opportunity to network, build relationships, and showcase your product or service.

4. Ask for referrals: Referrals are a powerful source of leads. Ask your existing customers for referrals and offer incentives for successful referrals.

5. Use cold calling and email: Cold calling and email may seem outdated, but they can still be effective if done correctly. Make sure to personalize your message and highlight the value of your product or service.

Prospecting requires patience, persistence, and a willingness to try new strategies. Not every prospect will turn into a customer, but by continually prospecting, you'll build a pipeline of leads that can convert into sales.

In conclusion, prospecting is a critical step in the sales process. By defining your target audience, using social media, attending events, asking for referrals, and using cold calling and email, you can identify and qualify potential customers. Remember to stay patient, persistent, and open to new strategies, and you'll build a solid foundation for successful sales.

CHAPTER 4

Qualifying Prospects

Qualifying prospects is the process of determining whether a potential customer is a good fit for your product or service. This step is important because it saves you time and resources by focusing on prospects who are most likely to buy.

Here are some effective strategies for qualifying prospects:

1. Use a lead scoring system: A lead scoring system assigns points to prospects based on their level of engagement and interest in your product or service. This can help you prioritize your follow-up and focus on prospects who are most likely to convert.

2. Ask the right questions: When engaging with potential customers, ask open-ended questions that uncover their needs, pain points, and buying habits. This will help you determine whether they are a good fit for your product or service.

3. Determine budget and decision-making authority: Qualifying prospects also involves determining their budget and decision-making authority. This will help you understand whether they have the resources to buy and whether they have the power to make a purchasing decision.

4. Evaluate timing: Timing is also an important factor in qualifying prospects. Determine whether the prospect is ready to buy now, or whether they are in the early stages of the buying process.

5. Address objections: Objections are a natural part of the sales process. Addressing objections and providing solutions can help you determine whether a prospect is a good fit for your product or service.

Qualifying prospects requires a combination of skills, including active listening, asking the right questions, and understanding customer needs. By implementing a lead scoring system, asking the right questions, determining budget and decision-making authority, evaluating timing, and addressing objections, you can effectively qualify prospects and focus on those who are most likely to convert into customers.

In conclusion, qualifying prospects is a critical step in the sales process. By determining whether a potential customer is a good fit for your product or service, you can save time and resources and focus on prospects who are most likely to buy.

CHAPTER 5
Building Rapport

Building rapport is the process of establishing a connection and developing a relationship with your potential customer. This step is crucial in the sales process because people buy from people they like and trust.

Here are some effective strategies for building rapport:

1. Be genuinely interested: Show a genuine interest in your potential customer by asking open-ended questions about their needs, goals, and challenges. Listen actively and show that you care about their success.

2. Find common ground: Look for common ground between you and your potential customer, whether it's a shared interest, a similar background, or a mutual connection. This can help build a sense of rapport and make the conversation more comfortable.

3. Use humor: Humor is a powerful tool for building rapport, as it can help break down barriers and make the conversation more enjoyable. Use humor sparingly and appropriately, and make sure it aligns with the tone of the conversation.

4. Show empathy: Empathy is the ability to understand and share the feelings of another person. Show empathy by acknowledging your potential customer's challenges and offering solutions that address their needs.

5. Be authentic: Authenticity is key to building rapport. Be yourself and avoid using scripted or canned responses. People can sense when someone is being fake, so be genuine and authentic in your interactions.

Building rapport takes time and effort, but it's worth it in the long run. By establishing a connection and developing a relationship with your potential customer, you increase the chances of them not only buying from you but also referring you and becoming a repeat customer!

In conclusion, building rapport is a critical step in the sales process. By showing a genuine interest, finding common ground, using humor, showing empathy, and being authentic, you can establish a connection and develop a relationship with your potential customer. Remember, people buy from people they like and trust.

CHAPTER 6

Presenting Your Offer

Presenting your offer is the moment of truth in the sales process. It's the point where you showcase your product or service and persuade your potential customer to take action. Here are some effective strategies for presenting your offer:

1. Focus on benefits, not features: Instead of listing features, focus on the benefits that your product or service can provide to your potential customer. Highlight how your offer can solve their challenges and help them achieve their goals. Stop selling a product and start selling a solution!

2. Use social proof: Social proof is the idea that people are influenced by the actions of others. Use social proof by showcasing customer testimonials, case studies, and success stories that demonstrate how your product or service has helped others.

3. Address objections: Addressing objections is a critical part of presenting your offer. Listen to your potential customer's concerns and provide solutions that address their objections. This shows that you understand their challenges and are willing to work with them to find a solution.

4. Offer alternatives: Offer alternative solutions if your potential customer isn't completely sold on your initial offer. This shows that you are flexible and willing to work with them to find a solution that meets their needs.

5. Create urgency: Creating a sense of urgency can motivate your potential customer to take action. Offer limited-time promotions or highlight the consequences of delaying a decision.

6. Close the sale: Finally, ask for the sale. Make a clear and specific request for them to take action, whether it's signing a contract, placing an order, or scheduling a follow-up call. The majority of sales that fall through are because the sales person never asked.

Presenting your offer requires a combination of persuasion, communication, and empathy. By focusing on benefits, using social proof, addressing objections, offering alternatives, creating urgency, and closing the sale, you can effectively present your offer and close more deals.

In conclusion, presenting your offer is the most important part of the sales process. By following these strategies, you can effectively showcase your product or service and persuade your potential customer to take action. Remember, selling is about helping your client solve a problem.

CHAPTER 7

Following Up

Following up is a critical part of the sales process that is often overlooked. It's essential to maintain contact with your potential customer after presenting your offer to keep the conversation going and increase the chances of closing the sale. Here are some effective strategies for following up:

1. Have a plan: Have a follow-up plan in place before presenting your offer. This includes knowing when and how you will follow up, and what you will say in each follow-up conversation.

2. Be persistent, but not pushy: Persistence is key to successful follow-up, but avoid being pushy or aggressive. Respect your potential customer's time and space, and focus on providing value in each follow-up conversation.

3. Provide value: Provide value in each follow-up conversation by sharing additional resources, offering insights, or addressing any new concerns or questions that may have arisen.

4. Use multiple channels: Use multiple channels to follow up, such as phone calls, emails, or social media messages. This

increases the chances of reaching your potential customer and maintaining contact.

5. Set expectations: Set clear expectations with your potential customer about when and how you will follow up. This shows that you are organized and committed to maintaining contact.

6. Stay positive: Stay positive and optimistic in each follow-up conversation, even if you haven't received a response. Remember that following up is a long-term strategy that requires patience and persistence.

Following up is an ongoing process that requires time and effort. By having a plan, being persistent, providing value, using multiple channels, setting expectations, and staying positive, you can effectively follow up and increase the chances of closing the sale.

In conclusion, following up is a critical part of the sales process that is often overlooked. By following these strategies, you can maintain contact with your potential customer and increase the chances of closing the sale. Remember, selling is about building relationships, and following up is an essential part of that process. We've all heard it, "The fortune is in the follow-up" and this couldn't be more true.

CHAPTER 8

Upselling and Cross-selling

Upselling and cross-selling are powerful techniques that can increase revenue and customer loyalty. Upselling involves offering a higher-priced version of the same product or service, while cross-selling involves offering complementary or related products or services. Here are some effective strategies for upselling and cross-selling:

1. Understand your customer's needs: Before attempting to upsell or cross-sell, understand your customer's needs and preferences. This helps you offer products or services that are relevant and valuable to them.

2. Position the upgrade or additional product as a benefit: Position the upgrade or additional product as a benefit that addresses your customer's specific needs or challenges. Highlight how the upgrade or additional product can provide more value or solve more problems than the original product or service.

3. Use social proof: Use social proof to demonstrate how the upgrade or additional product has benefited other customers. Share testimonials, case studies, or success stories that show how other customers have

achieved greater results with the upgraded or additional product.

4. Offer incentives: Offer incentives such as discounts or bonuses for upgrading or adding additional products or services. This can motivate your customer to take action and increase their perceived value.

5. Make it easy: Make it easy for your customer to upgrade or add additional products or services. Streamline the process and provide clear instructions on how to take advantage of the offer.

6. Follow up: Follow up with your customer after the upsell or cross-sell to ensure they are satisfied and address any concerns or issues they may have.

Upselling and cross-selling can be effective strategies for increasing revenue and customer loyalty. By understanding your customer's needs, positioning the upgrade or additional product as a benefit, using social proof, offering incentives, making it easy, and following up, you can effectively implement these strategies and achieve greater sales success.

In conclusion, upselling and cross-selling are powerful techniques that can increase revenue and customer loyalty. By following these strategies, you can effectively implement these techniques and achieve greater sales success. Remember, selling is about providing value to your customers, and upselling and cross-selling can provide additional value that meets their needs and preferences.

CHAPTER 9

Negotiation Strategies

Negotiation is a critical part of the sales process, and effective negotiation strategies can help you close more deals and achieve better outcomes. Here are some effective negotiation strategies to consider:

1. Prepare: Preparation is key to successful negotiation. Research your customer's needs, preferences, and budget, as well as your competitors and their offers. This helps you understand your customer's position and anticipate their objections or concerns.

2. Set clear goals: Set clear goals for the negotiation, such as price, delivery time, or product features. This helps you stay focused and avoid getting sidetracked by irrelevant issues.

3. Focus on value: Focus on the value that your product or service provides, rather than price alone. Highlight the benefits and outcomes that your customer can expect to achieve, and use this to justify your offer.

4. Use the "anchoring" technique: Use the "anchoring" technique by making an initial offer that is higher than your desired outcome. This sets a higher reference point

for the negotiation and makes your desired outcome seem more reasonable by comparison.

5. Listen actively: Listen actively to your customer's concerns and objections, and address them directly. This shows that you understand their needs and are committed to finding a solution that meets their requirements.

6. Offer alternatives: Offer alternatives that meet your customer's needs and preferences, even if they are different from your original offer. This shows that you are flexible and willing to work with your customer to find a mutually beneficial solution.

7. Know your walk-away point: Know your walk-away point, or the point at which you are willing to walk away from the negotiation. This helps you avoid making concessions that are not in your best interest.

Negotiation is a complex process that requires skill and practice. By preparing, setting clear goals, focusing on value, using the "anchoring" technique, listening actively, offering alternatives, and knowing your walk-away point, you can effectively negotiate and achieve better outcomes.

In conclusion, negotiation is a critical part of the sales process, and effective negotiation strategies can help you close more deals and achieve better outcomes. By following these strategies, you can negotiate effectively and achieve greater sales success. Remember, negotiation is about finding a solution that meets both your needs and your customer's needs, and these strategies can help you do just that.

CHAPTER 10

Developing a Sales Mindset

Developing a sales mindset is essential to achieving success in sales. A sales mindset is a set of beliefs, attitudes, and habits that help you stay motivated, focused, and resilient in the face of challenges and rejection. Here are some key elements of a sales mindset:

1. Believe in your product or service: To sell effectively, you must believe in your product or service and its ability to meet your customer's needs. This belief helps you communicate with confidence and enthusiasm and inspires trust and confidence in your customer. Be a product of your product.

2. Focus on your customer's needs: Focus on your customer's needs and preferences, rather than your own goals or agenda. This helps you provide value and build trust and rapport with your customer.

3. Embrace rejection: Rejection is an inevitable part of sales, but it can also be a source of motivation and learning. Embrace rejection as an opportunity to learn and improve, and use it to refine your approach and better understand your customer's needs.

4. Develop resilience: Develop resilience by maintaining a positive attitude and staying focused on your goals, even in the face of setbacks and challenges. This helps you stay motivated and persistent, and overcome obstacles and objections.

5. Continuous learning: Commit to continuous learning and improvement by seeking feedback, attending training, and staying up-to-date on industry trends and best practices. This helps you stay competitive and adapt to changing customer needs and preferences.

6. Take ownership: Take ownership of your results and actions, and hold yourself accountable for achieving your goals. This helps you take control of your success and stay focused on the things that matter most.

Developing a sales mindset takes time and effort, but it is essential to achieving success in sales. By believing in your product or service, focusing on your customer's needs, embracing rejection, developing resilience, committing to continuous learning, and taking ownership, you can develop a mindset that helps you achieve your sales goals and build lasting customer relationships.

In conclusion, developing a sales mindset is essential to achieving success in sales. By embracing these key elements of a sales mindset, you can develop the beliefs, attitudes, and habits that help you stay motivated, focused, and resilient in the face of challenges and rejection. Remember, selling is about providing value to your customers and building lasting relationships, and a sales mindset can help you do just that.

CONCLUSION

In conclusion, sales is a critical aspect of business, and mastering the art of sales can lead to significant success and growth. This e-book has covered various aspects of sales, including prospecting, qualifying prospects, building rapport, presenting offers, following up, upselling and cross-selling, negotiation strategies, and developing a sales mindset.

To be successful in sales, it is essential to have a clear understanding of your customer's needs and preferences, be knowledgeable about your product or service, and have effective communication and negotiation skills. Additionally, developing a positive and resilient sales mindset is crucial to overcoming challenges and achieving success.

Sales is an ongoing process that requires dedication, hard work, and continuous learning. By implementing the strategies outlined in this e-book and committing to ongoing improvement, you can become a successful salesperson and achieve your business goals.

Remember, sales is about building long-lasting relationships with your customers

CONCLUSION

and providing value to them. By focusing on your customer's needs, communicating effectively, and developing a positive and resilient mindset, you can create meaningful connections with your customers and grow your business.

For more information or if you would like to join my coaching group scan the qr below.